HIP-HOP & R&B

Culture, Music & Storytelling

Pharrell

HIP-HOP & R&B

Culture, Music & Storytelling

MASON CREST
Lori Vetere

HIP-HOP & R&B
Pharrell

Culture, Music & Storytelling

Mason Crest
450 Parkway Drive, Suite D
Broomall, Pennsylvania 19008
(866) MCP-BOOK (toll free)

First printing
9 8 7 6 5 4 3 2 1

hardback: 978-1-4222-4183-7
series: 978-1-4222-4176-9
ebook: 978-1-4222-7625-9

Library of Congress Cataloging-in-Publication Data

Names: Vetere, Lori, author.
Title: Pharrell / Lori Vetere.
Description: Broomall, PA : Mason Crest, 2018. | Series: Hip-hop & R&B: culture, music & storytelling.
Identifiers: LCCN 2018020773 (print) | LCCN 2018020984 (ebook) | ISBN 9781422276259 (eBook) | ISBN 9781422241837 (hardback) | ISBN 9781422241769 (series)
Subjects: LCSH: Pharrell--Juvenile literature. | Rap musicians--United States--Biography--Juvenile literature. | Singers--United States--Biography--Juvenile literature.
Classification: LCC ML3930.W55 (ebook) | LCC ML3930.W55 V47 2018 (print) | DDC 782.421649092 [B] --dc23
LC record available at https://lccn.loc.gov/2018020773

Developed and Produced by National Highlights, Inc.
Editor: Susan Uttendorfsky
Interior and cover design: Annalisa Gumbrecht, Studio Gumbrecht
Production: Michelle Luke

QR CODES AND LINKS TO THIRD-PARTY CONTENT

CONTENTS

KEY ICONS TO LOOK FOR:

 Words to understand: These words with their easy-to-understand definitions will increase the reader's understanding of the text while building vocabulary skills.

 Sidebars: This boxed material within the main text allows readers to build knowledge, gain insights, explore possibilities, and broaden their perspectives by weaving together additional information to provide realistic and holistic perspectives.

 Educational videos: Readers can view videos by scanning our QR codes, providing them with additional educational content to supplement the text. Examples include news coverage, moments in history, speeches, iconic sports moments, and much more!

 Text-dependent questions: These questions send the reader back to the text for more careful attention to the evidence presented there.

 Research projects: Readers are pointed toward areas of further inquiry connected to each chapter. Suggestions are provided for projects that encourage deeper research and analysis.

Series of glossary of key terms: This back-of-the-book glossary contains terminology used throughout this series. Words found here increase the reader's ability to read and comprehend higher-level books and articles in this field.

Chapter 1

Pharrell's Career Highlights—A Life Committed to Music

P harrell Williams is a phenomenon of the universe. This multi-talented musician, record producer, singer, rapper, actor, film producer, fashion designer, educator, and philanthropist hit the ground running when he was a teen and has never looked back. As part of the music production duo The Neptunes, Pharrell created a unique sound that many R&B and hip-hop artists used, dating from the late 1990s.

He is a founding member of the 1999 funk-rock band NE*R*D. In 2003, Pharrell came out with his first solo single, *Frontin'*, followed by the release of IN MY MIND, his first solo album, in 2006. His meteoric rise to fame accelerated in 2013 when he hit number one on charts around the globe with the amazing soundtrack from the movie *Despicable Me 2*, including the blockbuster hit *Happy*.

Pharrell is passionate about many things in his life, including fashion and design. Two very successful fashion labels were co-founded by him—Ice Cream and Billionaire Boys Club—and he has collaborated with many other designers around the world. He is involved with educational charities and contributes much of his time and money to creating learning experiences that will help children and teens to grow up with good educations and have interesting careers.

In 2014, Pharrell became a coach on the TV singing competition show *The Voice*. In 2015, his children's picture book, *Happy*, was released and became an immediate fixture for many weeks on the *New York Times* Best Seller List. Last, but definitely not least, Pharrell married Helen Lasichanh, a model, at Coconut Grove's Kampong National Tropical Botanical Gardens in 2013. The couple has four children, an eight-year-old son named Rocket, and triplets that were born in January 2017!

This chapter includes highlights of the many musical contributions Pharrell has made to society and reveals how talented and creative he is, even though virtually all of the people who know him are impressed by his down-to-earth manner and humility.

Pharrell Williams Discography

IN MY MIND
(Released July 25, 2006)

Pharrell's first solo album burst onto the scene in the number three slot on the *Billboard* Top 200 Chart (the 200 most popular EPs and record albums in the United States). IN MY MIND sold over 142,000 copies in its very first week on the charts, and went on to sell almost 3 million copies. Despite its initial popular success, it received mixed reviews from music critics. They expected much more from this experienced songwriter, singer, and record producer. The album was nominated for a Grammy in the category of Best Rap Album in 2007, but it lost out to RELEASE THERAPY by Ludacris.

The two most critically acclaimed songs on this album were *Can I Have It Like That*, a duet with Gwen Stefani, and *Number One*, a collaboration with Kanye West.

Can I Have It Like That
(Released October 2005)

The lead single from the album IN MY MIND was more successful worldwide than it was in the United States. Pharrell did not use his trademark high voice here, but instead rapped using a throaty baritone. He talks about his lifestyle and his achievements while a grinding bass plays underneath.

Scan the code to watch *Can I Have It Like That*, one of the two most successful songs on Pharrell's first solo album

Scan the code to watch *Number One*, the second most successful song on Pharrell's first album

Collaborations

- *Keep It Playa*, featuring Slim Thug
- *That Girl*, featuring Snoop Dogg and Charlie Wilson
- *Stay with Me*, featuring Pusha T
- *Baby*, featuring Nelly
- *Skateboard P Presents Show You How to Hustle*, featuring Lauren London

GIRL
(Released March 03, 2014)

Pharrell's second album garnered much greater success and included the blockbuster hit *Happy* (from the soundtrack of *Despicable Me 2*), which sold over 14 million copies worldwide and holds the honor of ranking as a contender in the list of the best-selling singles of all time.

Three other follow-up singles from the album—*Come Get It Bae, Gust of Wind,* and *Marilyn Monroe*—have gone on to receive critical success. *Happy* held its high position on the *Billboard* charts for forty-seven weeks, peaking at number one on March 08, 2014.

Nelly

G I R L, classified as an upbeat, pop R&B album, was certified Platinum on the UK (United Kingdom) album charts.

Collaborations

- *Know Who You Are,* featuring Alicia Keys
- *Brand New,* featuring Justin Timberlake

The Neptunes

The Neptunes is a production company formed by Pharrell and his best friend, Chad Hugo. Their firm has been instrumental in creating unique sounds for hundreds of successful hip-hop and R&B artists. Considered by many to be among the most successful music producers in history, The Neptunes racked up twenty-four top-ten hits on the *Billboard* Hot 100 Chart starting in the late 1990s. They were ranked number one by *Billboard* in its 2009 list of the Top 10 Producers of the Decade, and number three on the 10 Greatest Hip-Hop Beats of All Time (greatest producers) in 2015. Dr. Dre got the number one spot and DJ Premier came in second.

The Neptunes have released a number of songs over the years that feature Pharrell. Their record label is called *Star Trak Entertainment*, which boasts artists such as Robin Thicke, Snoop Dogg, Slim Thug, and Clipse (brothers No Malice and Pusha T).

Scan the code to watch *Happy,* one of the best-selling singles of all time (and winner of Best Pop Solo Performance at the 57th Grammy Awards) from Pharrell's second album, G I R L

Scan to watch the music video for *Jamaica Way* from Beenie Man's 2000 album, ART AND LIFE

Neptune Original Songs and Remixes Featuring Pharrell

Superthug

(Released September 21, 1998)

This hip-hop single was released from N.O.R.E.'s self-named album. It rocketed to number one on quite a few *Billboard* charts, including the *Billboard* Hot Rap Singles Chart, as well as reaching number fifteen on the Hot R&B/Hip-Hop Songs Chart. *Superthug* topped out at number thirty-six on *Billboard's* Hot 100 and marked the first time that Pharrell and The Neptunes were singled out and praised for their production skills.

Jamaica Way

(Released June 29, 2000)

Beenie Man's ART AND LIFE album contained the original *Jamaica Way* as track number seven on the reggae fusion album. The Neptunes remixed it for Beenie Man, featuring Kelis and Pharrell. The remix was released on July 11, 2000, under the same name. ART AND LIFE received a Grammy in 2001 for the Best Reggae Album of the Year and sold over 400,000 copies.

The Call

(Released February 06, 2001)

The Backstreet Boys' 2001 album BLACK & BLUE contained the original track with the same name.

The Neptune remix—with the modified, slightly edited and enlarged rap of the original hip-hop and R&B song—was released on March 13, 2001, and was featured on 2001's compilation album, Now That's What I Call Music! 7. Pharrell and Chad were praised for adding raw vocal harmonies and a pounding bassline to what was originally run-of-the-mill gospel music.

Neptune Productions over the Years

Compilation Album:
The Neptunes Present...Clones
(Released August 19, 2003)

Four singles were featured on this album of eighteen tracks, including Snoop Dogg's *It Blows My Mind*. Clones was a number one debut on *Billboard's* Top 200 Chart, with 250,000 in first-week sales, but sales fell quickly. The RIAA (Recording Industry Association of America) certified this album Gold only thirty-five days after its release, on September 22.

Frontin'
(Released August 19, 2003)

This single from The Neptunes Present... Clones album marked Pharrell's very first solo effort. This combination of crisp percussion, a minimum of bass notes, a fully synthetic main melody, and Pharrell's high voice turned out to be a blockbuster hit. Jay-Z's guest vocals only

Jay-Z

added to the excitement around the single. It peaked at number five on the *Billboard* Hot 100 Chart and number one on the Hot R&B/Hip-Hop Songs Chart.

Light Your Ass on Fire
(Released August 19, 2003)

This hip-hop/ rap classic single features Pharrell and Busta Rhymes. It peaked at number twelve on *Billboard's* Hot Rap Songs Chart, number twenty-three on the Hot R&B/Hip-Hop Songs Chart, and number sixty-nine on the Hot 100 Chart.

NE*R*D

NE*R*D is a funk-rock band that was created in 1999 by the owners of The Neptunes, Pharrell and Chad Hugo, and their longtime friend Shay Haley. NE*R*D is a backronym—an invented phrase, either serious or humorous, that pretends to be the source behind a word that's an acronym—for No-one Ever Really Dies. The group's music is a combination of hip-hop, funk, pop, rock, and R&B. Their first album, IN SEARCH OF, sold over five 500,000 copies in the United States, and the RIAA certified it as Gold.

Their second album, FLY OR DIE, sold over 400,000 copies in the United States, but attained Gold status because 500,000 albums were shipped.

NE*R*D disbanded in 2005, but reunited in 2008 under The Neptunes' record label, Star Trak

Scan the code to watch the music video for *Frontin'*, featuring Jay-Z

Pharrell HIP HOP & R&B

Entertainment. Under that label, NE*R*D has released four albums of their own material so far.

In Search Of
(Released August 06, 2001)

In Search Of was originally released in Europe in 2001, but the band was not happy with its sound. They decided to rerecord the album, adding live instruments in a collaboration with rock band Spymob. When it was released a second time in 2002, In Search Of started out at number sixty-one on *Billboard's* Top 200 Album Chart, but only climbed five spots to peak at number fifty-six.

Even though it was a worldwide release, it did not achieve the success of previous productions of The Neptunes.

The lead single, *Lapdance*, peaked at number thirty-six on *Billboard's* weekly list of Hot Modern Rock Tracks and number eighty-four on their weekly chart of Hot R&B/Hip-Hop Songs.

Rock Star, the second single from In Search Of, was released July 29, 2002, and climbed to number thirty-six on *Billboard's* weekly Hot Modern Rock Tracks. This song discusses rock stars who are posers and those stars whose particular time of notoriety has passed. An edited version of this song was used in the 2002 game *NFL Fever* as its theme song.

Scan the code to watch the music video for *Rock Star* featuring NE*R*D!

FLY OR DIE
(Released March 23, 2004)

NE*R*D decided to learn to play their own instruments so they could perform the twelve tracks on this album live. FLY OR DIE debuted at number six on the *Billboard* Top 200 Chart, with a very respectable 119,000 copies sold in the first week. It went on to be certified Gold, with total sales of over 400,000 copies in the United States alone.

The top single, *She Wants to Move* (released March 09, 2004), rose to number five in the UK charts. On first listen, this song seems to be misogynistic, but in reality, it praises women and encourages them to act and move freely in the world. *She Wants to Move*, together with the single *Maybe*, received extensive airplay on VH1 Soul, now known as BET Soul.

Chad Hugo of NE*R*D, in an interview with *MTV News* in December 2003, said,

> *We're the ones playing the instruments live this time [on FLY OR DIE]. I just started playing guitar last year so I'm learning as we go. Pharrell's playing drums. [Last time] we didn't have time to learn certain instruments so we got Spymob to help us out.*

SEEING SOUNDS
(Released June 09, 2008)

NE*R*D put out their third album in June 2008 after taking a three-year break. During their time off, they played at a music festival in Sweden, performed before 40,000 people at the Floriana Granaries (Isle of MTV 2008), performed in Chicago at the House of Blues, and toured as one of the opening acts of the famous *Glow in the Dark Tour* with Kanye West. SEEING SOUNDS sold 80,000 copies in its first week, debuting on *Billboard's* Top 200 Chart at number seven, but rapidly faded after its initial success.

The two most successful singles from this album are *Everyone Nose (All the Girls Standing in the Line for the Bathroom)*, released May 13, 2008, and *Spaz*, which was eventually used by Microsoft in a TV commercial for their product Zune.

Scan the code to watch the music video for *She Wants to Move* featuring NE*R*D!

NOTHING
(Released November 02, 2010)

NE*R*D's fourth album NOTHING was released in November 2010. Pharrell said,

> So we thought why not make a timeless album that's kind of a time capsule, so ten years from now people look at that album and go, 'I remember that era. That's when the NOTHING album came out.' I just wanted to make some good music that would affect people in a good way.

Scan the code to watch the music video for *Everyone Nose (All the Girls Standing in the Line for the Bathroom)* featuring NE*R*D

Nelly Furtado

The album started off at number twenty-one on the *Billboard* 200 Chart and sold 20,000 copies in its first week, but it received mixed reviews from U.S. music critics. The lead single on NOTHING is *Hot n Fun*, featuring Nelly Furtado. After its release on June 17, 2010, it became a top-thirty hit in Belgium, Italy, and the UK. The second official single is titled *Hypnotize U* and was produced by Daft Punk.

Tours

Pharrell has participated in one headlining tour—coinciding with the release of his solo album—completed one tour with NE*R*D, and has made appearances on a number of other tours.

DEAR GIRL *Tour* (OR DEAR G I R L *Tour*)

This was the very first solo concert tour for Pharrell. It began on September 07, 2014, in the ITU Stadium in Istanbul, Turkey, and he went on to perform twenty-six concerts throughout Europe, ending up on October 16, 2014, at the Zénith de Paris in Paris, France. The tour featured opening acts Cris Cab and Foxes, while the set list consisted primarily of songs from his second solo studio album, G I R L.

Scan the code to watch the music video for *Hot n Fun* featuring Nelly Furtado!

An interesting tidbit about Pharrell emerged during this 2014 concert series. His tour rider (a list of items requested by the artist to be placed in his room) included one or two framed photos of Carl Sagan, his childhood hero. He also asked for super cold sodas, alkaline water, Pedialyte, Patrón tequila, gluten-free bread, grass-fed beef, Nilla Wafers, and a box of matches.

NE*R*D GLOW IN THE DARK *Tour*

The worldwide 2008 *Glow in the Dark Tour* was very successful. Kanye West was the headliner, and the shows featured NE*R*D, Rihanna, Lupe Fiasco, Nas, and Santigold. The trip started in Seattle on April 16, 2008, and ended up in Australia on December 07, 2008. There were sixty-two shows in all—thirty-four in North America—and the group of artists spent almost two months touring the United States. The next leg of the tour covered Canada, England, Mexico, Brazil, and then on to the rest of Latin America.

Santigold

Then there were three shows in Asia, and five performances in Australia and New Zealand. NE*R*D split from the group in Australia and New Zealand and did a separate tour in those two countries.

Noteworthy Song Productions

For over twenty-five years, many of the best known hip-hop, rap, and R&B artists have passed through Pharrell's production studio. Many people know that he wrote and produced a lot of the songs featured in the 2014 movie *Despicable Me 2*—in addition to the number one hit song *Happy*—but here are just a few of the most popular songs that you may not have known were produced by Pharrell.

Girls Dem Sugar, Beenie Man
(Released September 14, 2000)

I'm a Slave 4 U, Britney Spears
(Released September 24, 2001)

Girlfriend, 'N Sync
(Released April 15, 2002)

'N Sync's very last song.

Work It Out, Beyoncé
(Released June 11, 2002)

This was Beyoncé's very first solo song!

Hollaback Girl, Gwen Stefani
(Released March 15, 2005)

This history-making release was the first song to sell over 1 million digital downloads.

Say Something, Mariah Carey
(Released April 12, 2005).

This song featured Snoop Dogg and is memorable for its video, which was filmed in Paris. In it, Pharrell plays Mariah Carey's love interest.

Wanna Love You Girl, Robin Thicke
(Released August 09, 2005)

Scan here to watch the music video for *Say Something* by Mariah Carey, in which Pharrell plays the part of her boyfriend

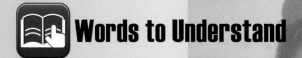

Words to Understand

aughts: a word to describe a century's first decade; most recently, the years from 2000–2009; not as accepted as "eighties" or "nineties" in describing a decade.

falsetto: a man singing in an unnaturally high voice, accomplished by creating a vibration at the very edge of the vocal chords.

sampler: a digital or electronic musical instrument, related to a synthesizer, that uses samples, or sound recordings, of real instruments (trumpet, violin, piano, etc.) mixed with excerpts of recorded songs and other interesting sounds (sirens, ocean waves, construction noises, car horns, etc.) that are stored digitally and can be replayed by a triggering device, like a sequencer, electronic drums, or a MIDI keyboard.

zeitgeist: a German word that means the defining mood or spirit of a particular age or time period; pronounced "zīt – gist."

Chapter 2:

Pharrell's Road to the Top

The Early Days

Pharrell Williams made his first appearance on Earth on April 05, 1973, in the city of Virginia Beach, Virginia. He was the oldest of three boys born to Carolyn Williams, a teacher and a librarian/media specialist who went on to earn four additional degrees, including a doctorate. His father was Pharaoh Williams, a handyman and house painter.

Dr. Carolyn Williams describes her son Pharrell as being "left-brained," which means that he is an out-of-the-box, creative thinker. His brother Cato was born in 1983, and Psolomon, his youngest brother, was born in 1993. Pharrell also has two half-brothers and two half-sisters from his father's previous marriage.

Although there was plenty of love in in the Williams's household growing up, there were times when it was difficult to pay the bills. "It wasn't, like, third world poverty, but let's just say we ate a lot of pork and beans," Pharrell's younger brother, David, said while NE*R*D was touring in Europe.

Pharrell did his part by working at McDonald's for a short time when he was a teenager. This job didn't last long, and neither did his jobs in two other restaurants. One of his supervisors, upon hearing that Pharrell was applying for a job in another fast-food restaurant, called them up to share this opinion: "Don't hire him! He burns the burgers and steals the nuggets."

After Mary Kaye Schilling interviewed Pharrell for a productivity article on FastCompany.com, she wrote,

> Growing up, Williams had no interest in how the world was presented to him, as hard rules or lines. As long as he can remember, he's wanted to blur them … Williams describes himself as a visual person, a kind of intelligence that isn't celebrated in most schools.

In her article, she quoted him as saying,

> The school system isn't spending a lot of time looking for specific potential. We are bred to be worker bees: to grow up, get married, have a kid, drive a Volvo, do our taxes, invest in something, find a hobby … I spent a lot of time in school not paying attention.

Musical Influences as a Child

What were some of Pharrell's musical influences growing up? In an interview with Oprah in 2014, he fondly remembered playing Follow the Leader on his bike and listening to the music people played outside of their apartments: Rufus and Chaka Khan, Luther Vandross, Stevie Wonder, even Axl Rose. At that time, Pharrell did not realize he has a special neurological condition called "synesthesia," which allows him to "see" sounds.

In an interview on *Nightline* in December 2012, Pharrell shared what the experience was like for him.

> *It just always stuck out in my mind, and I could always see it. I don't know if that makes sense, but I could always visualize what I was hearing … Yeah, it was always like weird colors.*

Band Camp and Marching Band

Pharrell credits his grandmother for getting him interested in playing drums and joining a marching band. As a child, he constantly gathered up spoons, pots, and pans and created makeshift drum sets. One day, when he was about to enter seventh grade, his grandmother said, "You like the drums, so why don't you learn?" That made sense and put him on the road to a career in music. That, of course, and the chords he heard on the very first A Tribe Called Quest album he bought.

He met his oldest friend and most frequent collaborator, Chad Hugo, in a school summer band camp for Virginia's Talented and Gifted Program in seventh grade. Hugo played the tenor sax and

Williams played drums and keyboard. In addition, they both were in a marching band—Chad was a drum major and Pharrell played the snare drum. The friends then marched into Princess Anne High School and continued to play in the school band.

It was during this time that Chad and Pharrell spent hours dissecting various Tribe songs, trying to pin down why the beats created certain emotions. It was a small jump from there to figuring out how to make their own tracks, and then another small jump to make tracks for Teddy Riley, the music producer who discovered them playing at a high school talent show.

Looking back, Pharrell cites being in school bands as responsible for giving him two important tools that he used to turn into success: discipline in the marching band drum-line—which he remembers as being almost military in nature—and the ability to read music.

The Start of a Professional Musical Career

The Neptunes

Fast-forward to the early 1990s, when Pharrell and Chad, still in high school, put together a four-piece R&B-style band called The Neptunes. Together with friends Mike Etheridge and Shay Haley, they decided to enter a talent show at their high school. It was a momentous occasion since they were "discovered" there by Teddy Riley, a record producer, singer, songwriter, and musician—who just happened to have a recording studio next door to the high school!

Teddy is considered to be an important influence on the evolution of hip-hop, pop, soul, and contemporary R&B music since the 1980s. As soon as both Pharrell and Chad graduated from high school, they signed a contract with him and became a production duo.

When asked whether he knows if a song is going to become a huge hit or not, Pharrell said,

> No sir, I don't know when a song is going to be huge—you never know really. The people make that decision. The only thing you can do is be loyal to your creativity and try to do something new and fresh, and leave it at that. What makes a song huge is people buying records, streaming it online, voting for it, and those are things that are out of my control. Those are the factors that make a song a hit; it's never been me. The people decide. What I do is such a small part. … A producer is the person that can either make a hit or break a hit.

Some of the first tracks The Neptunes produced for other musical artists include *Rump Shaker* and *New Jack Swing Pt. II* for Wreckx N' Effect in 1992, and *Right Here* by SWV (Sisters with Voices) in 1993—both versions: the extended Human Nature mix that became a number one single in the United States, and the UK version featuring Pharrell.

Pharrell describes the kind of sound that he and Chad were working on as "minimalist" and "simplistic." They wanted to use as few sounds as possible, which was the opposite of what many musicians were doing at that time. The trend was working with a heaviness of sound.

Drop It Like It's Hot
by Snoop Dogg, featuring
Pharrell Williams
(Released September 12, 2004)

When written about on ETCanada.com, this Snoop Dogg cut of *Drop It Like It's Hot* was labeled as bringing back minimalism, thanks to Pharrell's production. The write-up described the inclusion of a **sampler** beat made just from tongue clicks, keyboards, and a drum machine. It is a perfect example of the sound Pharrell and Chad were going for when bringing their talent to the music industry. Thanks to Snoop, the phrase "Drop it like it's hot" joined the **zeitgeist**.

Scan to watch the music video for *Right Here* by SWV

The Neptunes' Reach

The Neptunes put their special touch on literally hundreds of songs and have garnered hits in practically every musical genre, relying on their extremely creative and absolutely exceptional beats. Nearly everyone who is anyone in the hip-hop world owes a great deal of gratitude to The Neptunes for producing the music for their albums, films, videos, commercials, award presentations, and so on.

The production duo mapped out beats for Justin Timberlake, Mary J. Blige, Babyface, Janet Jackson, R&B superstar Usher, rappers Jay-Z, Nelly, Ray J, Busta Rhymes, P. Diddy, Mystikal, Ludacris, Fabolous, and Ma$e, as well as for major rock acts Marilyn Manson, Garbage, Limp Bizkit, and No Doubt.

The Neptunes have combined rock guitar riffs, synthesizer beats, and snippets of sounds from 1980s pop culture, including the earliest cell phone ringtones and bleeps used by Atari. The combination of repetitive electronic arrangements and hooks with digital, flat, hard tones has contributed greatly to this duo's success. In fact, it was said that in 2013, The Neptunes had a creative hand in nearly 20 percent of British radio hits, and a whopping 43 percent of U.S. radio songs!

They achieved great success while producing such hits as *I Just Wanna Love U (Give It 2 Me)* in 2000 by Jay-Z and *U Don't Have to Call* by Usher in 2002. In 2003, they shot to worldwide fame by producing *I'm a Slave 4 U* by Britney Spears. Pharrell and Chad are also responsible for launching the meteoric career of Justin Timberlake. In fact, The Neptunes hold the number one position on *Billboard's* list of Top 10 Producers of the Decade for the **aughts** (2000s)!

Scan to watch the music video for *Drop It Like It's Hot* by Snoop Dogg

These very successful music producers—who started in the 1990s—are still creating music today. In 2017, they were estimated to be worth about $160 million and considered to part of a small group of the most successful producers in the history of music. Their sounds combine tones from Asian and Middle Eastern music, including woodwinds and percussion instruments with stripped-down electronic funk. Pharrell raps, sings, and appears in videos, while his partner Chad works behind the scenes.

NE*R*D

In 2002, Pharrell and Chad formed an American record label named Star Trak Entertainment. Originally signed as the duo forming The Neptunes, they then joined with old friend Shay Haley to form NE*R*D (No-one Ever Really Dies), a mostly funk-rock R&B hip-hop band. Pharrell provides the lead vocals and also plays the drums, piano, percussion, and keyboards.

For this trio, NE*R*D is more than just a name—it is also their philosophy on life. Writing on the band's website, Pharrell explained their philosophy this way:

> *People's energies are made of their souls. When you die, that energy may disperse, but it isn't destroyed. Energy cannot be destroyed. It can manifest in a different way but even then it's like their souls are going somewhere. If it's going to heaven or hell or even if it's going into a fog or somewhere in the atmosphere to lurk unbeknownst to itself, it's going somewhere.*

NE*R*D's albums—2002's IN SEARCH OF and 2004's FLY OR DIE—have a unique sound. It was created by first recording the album using synthesizers, and, afterward, rerecording the songs using a live band. The sound of guitars imitating synthesizers is fresh and different.

On November 01, 2017, NE*R*D released

What's it like to hear colors?

their first single in seven years. *Lemon* features Rihanna and is from their soon-to-be-released album No One Ever Really Dies.

Pharrell's Singing Voice

Much has been written about Pharrell's "feather-light vocal style" and his "iconic **falsetto**." The truth is that falsetto voices have played a gigantic part in the music industry, first in R&B music, Motown, and soul, and then in pop music and indie rock. Pharrell shows that he is the master of falsetto in songs like 2013's *Blurred Lines* by Robin Thicke and *Get Lucky by* Daft Punk.

Text-Dependent Questions:

❶ What made up some of the earliest beats that were used by The Neptunes?

❷ Who encouraged Pharrell to learn to play the drums?

❸ Who discovered Pharrell and Chad at a high school talent show?

Research Project:

In this chapter, Pharrell refers to a special neurological condition he has called "synesthesia," which allows him to "see" sounds. Research this particular condition, which is genetic and affects 4 percent of the population. Then pick a different musician who also has this condition, and compare his or her symptoms to those experienced by Pharrell. Some examples of musicians who have synesthesia are Tori Amos, Duke Ellington, Billy Joel, Dev Hynes, Patrick Stump, and Charli XCX.

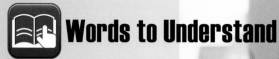 **Words to Understand**

athleisure: a fashion trend in which traditional workout clothing is upgraded to be worn fashionably at school, in the workplace, or at casual social occasions: leggings, tights, yoga pants, hooded or zip-front sweatshirts, and sneakers.

endorsement: money earned from a product recommendation, typically by a celebrity, athlete, or other public figure.

jingle: a short verse, tune, or slogan used in advertising to make a product easily remembered.

titanium: a hard silver or gray metal used in corrosion-resistant alloys because it is light and strong.

Chapter 3:

Pharrell's Other Interests and Passions

Movie and Television Soundtracks

Pharrell has 118 credits on IMDb, the official Internet Movie Database, for his work as a writer, performer, or producer of movie soundtracks, and an astonishing 174 credits for being a writer or performer on a television series. For example, he wrote sixteen episodes of *The Tonight Show Starring Jimmy Fallon* from 2014–2017 and performed four times—earning four credits—on the same show during 2015–2016. He also wrote original songs and themes for the movies *Despicable Me* (2010), *Despicable Me 2* (2013), *Despicable Me 3* (2017), and *The Amazing Spider-Man 2* (2014).

Christopher Meledandri and Pharrell Williams at the 25th Annual Producers Guild Awards held at the Beverly Hilton Hotel in Los Angeles, CA on January 19, 2014

A Sampling of Soundtracks

Despicable Me 2
(Released July 03, 2013)

Pharrell wrote five of the full-length songs for the movie *Despicable Me 2*, and performed four. The song *Happy* exploded from the soundtrack onto the world stage, and people could not get enough of the original video. It made everyone happy and made them want to dance in the streets as well.

To meet the demand, Pharrell created a website—24hoursofhappy.com—which turned into a global first. Filmed in Los Angeles, the video captures four-minute segments of people dancing in the street to the song, totaling twenty-four hours of nonstop Happy-ness.

The craze continued, and soon, people were shooting their own *Happy* videos all over the world, including Iran, where participants in the video were arrested for defying Iran's traditional behavior code.

SpongeBob Movie: Sponge out of Water
(Released January 28, 2015)

Pharrell wrote and produced three out of the five songs released on the movie's soundtrack: *Squeeze Me, Sandy Squirrel,* and *Patrick Star*. These were different tunes than the official musical score for the film.

Hidden Figures
(Released December 25, 2016)

Pharrell composed and produced the music for this dramatic film detailing the little-known history of three African-American women who played a significant part in NASA's role of helping to launch astronaut John Glenn into orbit.

"I'm Lovin' It"

For many years, people have reported that Pharrell both co-wrote and produced the extremely popular and catchy McDonald's **jingle** "I'm Lovin' It," sung by Justin Timberlake. This fact was discredited in June 2016 when Steve Stoute, a former record executive, claimed in an interview that rapper Pusha T, half of the historic hip-hop duo Clipse, wrote the jingle in 2004.

Pusha T

Video Game Soundtracks

Beginning in 2002, Pharrell has either written for or performed in ten video games so far, including *Madden NFL 18* (2017), *Grand Theft Auto IV and V* (2008 and 2013), *Despicable Me: Minion Rush* (2013), and *Dance Paradise* (2010–2011).

More Than a Singer and a Music Producer

Actor

Along with his extremely busy career as a composer, singer, and producer, somehow Pharrell has found the time to appear in four films: *Popstar: Never Stop Never Stopping* (as himself) (2016); *Entourage* (as himself) (2015); *Pitch Perfect 2* (as the voice judge) (2015); and *Get Him to the Greek* (as himself) (2010).

He has two credits for acting on television: *Shining a Light: A Concert for Progress On Race in America*, a made-for-television movie (2015), and an episode of the TV series *90210*, where he appeared with NE*R*D (2009). He has also appeared as himself in 159 TV shows, 12 documentaries, 9 videos, and 5 short films!

Coach

In 2014–2015, Pharrell appeared as a coach on the seventh season of *The Voice*. In a 2013 interview for FastCompany.com, he explained his appearance choices to Mary Kaye Schilling.

> **❝** *Most anything I do I do because it involves someone I can learn from … Sometimes you just gotta put your pride aside and be quiet so that you can absorb not only what a person is saying but how they are saying it—their energy, their body language. It's all for a reason.* **❞**

Movie Producer

Sean "Puffy" Combs

Pharrell turned his hand to movie production in 2015 when he became an executive producer of the film *Dope*, along with Sean Combs (aka Sean "Puffy" Combs). The crime-comedy-drama film starred Shameik Moore, Tony Revolori, Kiersey Clemons, Blake Anderson, Zoë Kravitz, A$AP Rocky, and Chanel Iman, and received positive views from critics.

Scan to watch the video introduction of Pharrell's YouTube channel

Music-Related Business Ventures

i am OTHER

This multimedia creative collection was started by Pharrell in 2012. He combines all of his fashion and environmental endeavors, and those of other designers around the world, into programming under the umbrella of his own YouTube channel. Pharrell says the channel is "a cultural movement dedicated to Thinkers, Innovators, and Outcasts."

Interestingly, will.i.am took Pharrell to court in 2013 for trademark infringement because the phrase "i am," he felt, was too close to I.Am.Symbolic, will.i.am's brand company name. They settled the case out of court after six months.

Marketing and Designing Clothes and Other Accessories

Pharrell approaches life with enthusiasm, taste, and creativity. That not only includes the music industry, but the world of fashion as well. The artist combined his love of design with the world of fashion and, like everything else he does, came out a winner.

Fashion Lines

Billionaire Boys Club (BBC) and Ice Cream

The famous Japanese designer who created Bathing Ape streetwear, Nigo (Tomoaki "Nigo" Nagao), and Pharrell created the Billionaire Boys Club fashion line in 2005. Their streetwear consists of hip-hop-, artist-, and skater-inspired footwear, t-shirts, sweatshirts, polos, pants, jackets, hats, outerwear, and accessories.

A Billionaire Girls Club was established in December 2011.

Who is a Member of the BBC?

In a 2013 interview for Complex.com, Pharrell explained,

❝[The Billionaire Boys Club] was born in Japan, and the people who belong in this club are the people who are like-minded, who know that education is one of the greatest gifts to life, and learning things and continuing to discover and explore is one of the greatest experiences we can ever have as humans. So, it's anyone who believes that and lives their life to the fullest.❞

Athleisure Wear

The **athleisure** trend became popular in 2016 and 2017, and of course, Pharrell is right at the top of designing combination sportswear, work, and evening wear all rolled up into incredibly comfortable outfits, pairs of sneakers, or stretchy accessories that can be worn all day long.

G-Star Raw

In 2015, Pharrell launched his third fashion collection with Bionic Yarn, which makes denim clothing out of recycled plastic that has been retrieved from the oceans. The fabrics have been developed in conjunction with Bionic Yarn.

Sunglasses and Jewelry

In 2013, Pharrell designed a line of three bold unisex sunglasses constructed of **titanium** for Moncler. The glasses are futuristic, use clean traditional lines, and have steampunk influences.

Furniture Design

Pharrell has designed chairs with French manufacturer Domeau & Pérès and Emmanuel Perrotin, a talented French art dealer who is interested in contemporary art. One chair Pharrell designed in 2008 features a molded plastic seat atop human legs. In 2009, he designed chairs that featured clear tank wheels instead of legs.

Sculpture

A collaborative sculpture titled *Simple Things* was unveiled in 2009. The two creating artists were Pharrell Williams and Takashi Murakami. *Simple Things* is constructed of fiber, steel, acrylic, wood, LED lights, and seven objects made of white, yellow, and

Pharrell Williams and Takashi Murakam

pink gold set with rubies, sapphires, emeralds, and diamonds. There's a small bottle of Heinz Ketchup, a shoe from the Billionaire Boys Club label, a little bag of Doritos, and a cupcake— all iced out with jewels.

Pharrell said of this strange object, "It's made with 26,000 diamonds and gems … I wanted people to see the value of simple things with some of the staples of American culture."

Endorsements

Pharrell is an extremely popular celebrity, and so an **endorsement** from him is very valuable in today's advertising world. Here is a partial list of endorsements that Pharrell has made.

Adidas

Pharrell signed with Adidas in 2014 and continues working with them in 2017. When he first started working with them, Pharrell talked about how he grew up wearing their classic tracksuits, as well as Stan Smith sneakers.

Beats by Dre

Along with eighteen other public figures, Pharrell endorsed Apple's wireless ear pieces in a 2016 commercial. All the celebs were

Scan to watch the music video for *Beats by Dre Presents: Got No Strings*

featured using Apple's headphones BeatsX, Powerbeats 3 Wireless, or Beats Solo3 Wireless while listening to Disney's Pinocchio singing *I've Got No Strings.*

Billionaire Boys Club

Pharrell's clothing line is extremely popular with fans, as well as with peers like Jay-Z. The Club endorses Adidas' Stan Smith sneakers, which feature BBC's Diamonds and Dollars print.

Bionic Yarn

Bionic Yarn and Pharrell, under his Adidas line, began recycling plastic gathered from the ocean bottoms and transforming it into chic, wearable clothing. Pharrell named this fashion collection G-Star Raw.

Chanel

On October 26, 2017, Pharrell announced that, in collaboration with Adidas, he had designed a one-of-a-kind sneaker that will be soon introduced by Chanel. Rumor has it that the shoes are white and black trainers that have the word "Chanel" written along one shoe's front, and the word "Pharrell" written along the other shoe's front, in capital letters.

Awards Won

Pharrell has won numerous accolades over the years, and has been nominated for many more! What follows is only a partial listing of musical awards for solo work, collaborations, for his work as producer with The Neptunes, and as a member of NE*R*D.

He has also won awards from the fashion industry, the film industry, and from *Time* (magazine).

Billboard Awards

R&B/Hip-Hop Producer of the Year—
The Neptunes | Won in 2003

R&B/Hip-Hop Producer of the Decade—
The Neptunes | Won in 2009

Top Hot 100 Song—*Blurred Lines*,
featuring Robin Thicke | Won in 2014

Top Digital Song—*Blurred Lines*,
featuring Robin Thicke | Won in 2014

Top R&B Song—*Blurred Lines*,
featuring Robin Thicke | Won in 2014

Top Radio Song—*Blurred Lines*,
featuring Robin Thicke | Won in 2014

Grammy Awards

Best Rap Song—*Alright*, featuring Sounwave,
Kawan Prather, and Kendrick Lamar | Won in 2016

Best Music Video—*Happy* | Won in 2015

Best Urban Contemporary Album—G I R L | Won in 2015

Best Pop Solo Performance—*Happy* | Won in 2015

Album of the Year—Random Access Memories,
featuring Daft Punk, et al. | Won in 2014

Record of the Year—*Get Lucky*,
featuring Nile Rodgers and Daft Punk | Won in 2014

Best Pop Duo/Group Performance—*Get Lucky*,
featuring Nile Rodgers and Daft Punk | Won in 2014

Best Rap Song—*Money Maker*,
featuring Ludacris | Won in 2007

ASCAP Film and Television Music Award

ASCAP Award, Top Box Office Films category—
score of *Despicable Me,* with Heitor Pereira | Won in 2011

BBC Music Awards

International Artist of the Year—*Happy* | Won in 2014
Song of the Year—*Happy* | Won in 2014

BET Awards

Best Hip-Hop Club Banger—*Move That Doh,* featuring Pusha T
and Casino | Won in 2014

Best Male R&B/Pop Artist | Won in 2013

Best Video of the Year—*Happy* | Won in 2014

Council of Fashion Designers of America (CFDA) Awards
Fashion Icon Award | Won in 2015

iHeartRadio Music Awards
Innovator Award | Won in 2014

NAACP Image Awards
Outstanding Song, Traditional—*I See Victory*,
featuring Kim Burrell | Won in 2017

Outstanding Male Artist | Won in 2015, 2016, and 2017

MTV Africa Music Awards
Best International Act—Pharrell Williams | Won in 2014

MTV Video Music Awards
Best Male Video—*Sing*, featuring Ed Sheeran | Won in 2014

People's Choice Award
USA, Favorite R&B Artist | Won in 2015

Time (magazine)
100 Most Influential People in the World Award | Won in 2014

World Soundtrack Award
Best Original Song Written Directly for a Film—
Despicable Me 2, Happy | Won in 2013

Text-Dependent Questions:

❶ How many Grammy Awards has Pharrell won?

❷ What are the names of two important fashion lines created by Pharrell?

❸ What is athleisure wear?

Research Project:

Pharrell can be described as a "Renaissance Man," or a person who is well-rounded, versatile, and an expert in many different areas. Choose one of Pharrell's many interests outside of the music industry and research it. What has he contributed to that field? Explain why you think Pharrell was drawn to that particular field, and what might have influenced him along the path to success?

📖 Words to Understand

lossless: a computing term for compressing data without losing any information— preferred whenever it's important that the original data file and a decompressed data file be identical.

opine: to state or express an opinion.

rampant: spreading unchecked or uncontrolled in any way.

resonate: to be filled with or produce a full, deep, reverberating sound; to evoke a feeling of shared emotion or belief.

Chapter 4:

Building a Brand, Marketing, and Messaging

Marketing His Brand

I t's no secret that Pharrell is a genius, not only in the various realms of the music field (composing, producing, and singing), but in the world of digital marketing as well. He has created a number of brands, including Ice Cream and the Billionaire Boys Club (BBC), that **resonate** with his fans. They are eager to purchase his music and any products associated with his name.

The World's First 24-Hour Music Video

The blockbuster hit of 2013, the song *Happy*, made for an insanely successful year for Pharrell. The original video was already garnering millions of hits, but Pharrell decided more could be done with the huge number of the song's fans. So he came up with the idea of creating "the world's first 24-hour music video."

The original song played repeatedly on a loop while hundreds of Los Angeles,

California, celebrities and regular people danced and lip-synched the words in the street. The concept of sharing the dancing with fans was so successful that the web page containing the twenty-four hours of video has received almost 58 million views at the time of this writing!

You can also watch twenty-four individual Pharrell *Happy* videos here—an hour-long video for each hour of the day! https://www.youtube.com/playlist?list=PLKPi39tTpkdpjBVQZo5oFLWjFjlOMkd2A.

Lyrical Messages to the World and to His Fans

There's no doubt about it—lyrics are an important part of most songs. Let's say you're chilling in your room, maybe checking out some videos on YouTube. The first thing that may attract you is the music and the beat. You decide to replay the song, this time listening to the lyrics. Sometimes the words speak to you in a way that resonates. You think, *He's saying exactly what I'm thinking* or *She knows what it means to struggle.* In that moment, you feel a kinship with the singer as the words touch your soul.

Lyrics can be modern-day poetry. On the other hand, some lyrics are just words—words that fit with a particular beat, a certain sound. It's easy to tell the difference. Pharrell's lyrics are a mixture of the two types of lyrics, although it's easy to see that right from the beginning of his career, he wanted to share a message of hope with his followers.

Early Pharrell gives good advice to his audience. Then Pharrell goes through doubt and depression and a bit of rage and comes out on the other side a philosopher, a person who tells you how to live if you want to get through times of depression and craziness. In

contrast, *Happy* wants its listeners to feel free, to be able to dance in the streets and express their happiness.

What Is Pharrell's Net Worth?

This master at writing, singing, performing, producing, and creating music is also a master at forming very successful businesses, ranging from the music industry to the world of fashion to art to jewelry to— Well, you get the picture. How wealthy is he?

According to estimates from late 2016, Pharrell has a net worth of approximately $150 million—and that is probably a conservative figure. You might ask yourself how he achieved that level of success in so many areas. One answer is that he is constantly active and takes care of his health. Another component to his success is that he uses tried-and-true methods to connect with his audience.

Every time the master gets a message across in a song, whether online, on the radio, on TV, or in a video, he is building his brand. He also keeps fans' interest high in his career by doing interviews, guest appearances, tours, press conferences, and attending charity events. He is a great philanthropist, which you'll find out about in Chapter 5.

Social media (Facebook, Twitter, and Instagram) lets him connect with his fan base, try out new ideas, and so on. He uses advertising to catch people's interest in his new fashion designs, and to discover his collaborations with companies and artists around the world. For instance, he has a huge fan base in Japan.

There's nothing like an interesting video to get an idea across, as well as to market a brand. Pharrell has participated in hundreds of interviews over the years, from talk shows to TV to online appearances. Through it all, he comes across as a highly intelligent, humble, and caring person.

These are a few of the interviews that made a mark in this age of media saturation:

- 2003—Michael Jackson interviewed Pharrell Williams
- 2012—Pharrell and Quincy Jones shared a joint interview for PopStopTV.com
- 2013—Pharrell was interviewed at the *GQ* Men of the Year Awards
- 2014—Pharrell provided an interview to *The Telegraph* to promote his appearance at the London Finsbury Park Wireless Festival
- 2015—Pharrell participated in an interview with Jason King of *NPR*
- 2016—Complex Sneakers interviewed Pharrell about his newest Adidas collaboration—a shoe called Hu that was inspired by North Dakota Native Americans
- 2017—Pirelli interviewed Pharrell, who said, "How can we inspire [other people] if we are only behind the scenes?"

The Power of Press Conferences

Just like many other celebrities, Pharrell understands the power that press conferences can have when launching a product. They are especially useful for letting an artist's audience know about new

projects being worked on, and they also give the artist a chance to **opine** on political views, current events, and so on. Press conferences often have an element of surprise about them, simply because the public's interest is attracted by surprise.

An example of a press conference that Pharrell conducted in recent years was in 2015, when he called a press conference to talk about his new children's book, *Happy*. It contains photos of children from many different cultures explaining what it means to them to be happy. The twist in this press conference was that he was interviewed by an audience full of children.

In December 2016, a press event was held to introduce the film *Hidden Figures*. Pharrell produced this movie, which dramatizes the true, never-before-told story of a group of brilliant African-American women who contributed to America's ability to win the space race with Russia—to be the first country to have astronauts orbit the globe.

Talking to the Radio Waves

Pharrell, along with friend and music supervisor Scott Vener, are hosts of a two-hour biweekly show on Drake's *Beats 1* radio station called *OTHERtone*. The show features "newness, freshness, and what-is-that-ness" for its listeners. A subscription to Apple Music is required to hear the program.

The World of Social Media

Facebook

Almost 11 million people follow Pharrell on Facebook. NE*R*D's official page has almost 415,000 likes and 400,000 followers. All of Pharrell's followers are treated to thousands of timeline photos, where his many interests are displayed and discussed. Fans are often directed to Pharrell's official web page.

NE*R*D's page advertises upcoming events and directs fans to its official website. The only Facebook section that has any real updated content on NE*R*D's page is where public posts and photos can be added.

In 2017, there was a lot of speculation that NE*R*D might be about to release their first new album in seven years. Hope was **rampant**, since NE*R*D signs appeared in various locations after a complete purge of all their social media accounts in early 2017.

Fans were right, as a new album entitled No One Ever Really Dies is to be released in December 2017.

Twitter

Pharrell has 10.6 million followers on Twitter who have eagerly read his over four thousand tweets. Since July 2011 alone, he has tweeted news, publicity, and over seven hundred videos and photos.

For instance, Pharrell revealed NE*R*D's new album cover art and release date via Instagram and Twitter on November 22, 2017.

Twitter is the perfect quick-and-easy venue for Pharrell to alert his fans to new and innovative ideas. He uses it to recommend fresh music available on iTunes, Apple Music, Google Play, Spotify, Tidal, Napster, and other sites. He also retweets noteworthy comments from Rihanna, LeBron James, Barack Obama, Adidas, and many others.

Frequently, Pharrell's tweets contain encouraging statements, such as this one from August 26, 2017: "Stand for what you stand in. If you see the potential for good, speak up. Don't be Quiet. @Fam1stfam #adidasPharrellWilliams."

Instagram

Pharrell's 10.2 million followers on Instagram enjoy his use of this venue to encourage his friends and the public at large. An example is this post from October 06, 2017: "The lyrical genius that is @blackthought and the timeless legendary music of the Roots. My mind is blown."

YouTube

There are literally hundreds of Pharrell videos on YouTube. Fans can locate lists of videos, playlists, and channels by searching "Pharrell Williams—Topic." His videos most frequently appear on his *i am OTHER* channel, which currently boasts almost 1.8 million subscribers. Pharrell created this cultural meeting place and dedicated it to "Thinkers, Innovators, and Outcasts."

From the *i am OTHER* channel, fans can access hundreds of relevant videos and videos from *Meet the Baes*, which is a series introducing fans to singers and dancers who have performed on the stage alongside Pharrell.

His *OTHERtone* channel contains videos captured from interviews on *Beats 1*. There is also a section entitled "Stereo Types," where fans and people on the street are interviewed about their style, culture, musical taste, and opinions on race.

Spotify

Many fans access Pharrell's most popular music on Spotify, a digital music service that contains literally millions of tracks. Personalized playlists can be generated by signing up and paying a monthly subscription fee.

Tidal

Tidal is another music-streaming service that is subscription-based like Spotify, but it offers superior, **lossless** audio. It is owned by Pharrell's good friend, Jay-Z.

PharrellWilliams.com

In 2016, Pharrell developed a website that involves his fans

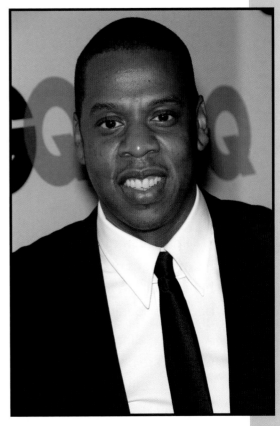

Jay-Z

in his creation processes. Users are encouraged to log in to www.pharrellwilliams.com from Facebook and create a fan card.

A person can select one of five different categories—music, art and design, fashion, social good, or TV and film—and pick their personal favorite project contained within that category. Then they upload their personalized, unique card on to the main home page. Every time they access the site, their personal preferences become the entry point.

It can be confusing for a new user to go to Pharrell's website and see a bunch of colored squares with the names and photos of a lot of unknown fans, but Pharrell is nothing if not creative, and we're certain that there must be some hidden advantages to setting up his website in this manner.

The site mentions that the shared home page is the perfect place to access exclusive tracks, tour updates, behind-the-scenes content, and live events.

Award Speeches

Pharrell frequently uses heartfelt acceptance speeches to get his messages of fighting social injustice, gender inequality, and hate speech in all forms across to his audience. He has recently begun to speak out about empowering women.

An excellent example of his thoughts on what can happen if women are not held back is contained in his remarks at the 185th commencement of New York University in May 2017. Pharrell was the main speaker at Yankee Stadium in front of approximately 3,000 people, where he received an honorary doctorate of fine arts degree for his work as a producer, songwriter, and musician.

> *Speaking to you guys today has me charged up. As you find your ways to serve humanity, it gives me great comfort knowing this generation is the first that understands that we need to lift up our women. Imagine the possibilities when we remove imbalance from the Ether. Imagine the possibilities when women are not held back. Your generation is unraveling deeply entrenched laws, principles and misguided values that have held women back for far too long and, therefore, have held us ALL back. The world you will live in will be better for it.*

Pharrell also gave a short but heartfelt speech about embracing nonconformity when he performed his song *Freedom* at 2015's MTV Video Music Awards.

"They tried to put us in a box. They tried to categorize us. Tonight, we change things. We will express ourselves and let all of that go."

What Can We Learn from Pharrell?

Diversified Talents

One of the most important lessons he teaches us is that we can't be good at just one thing. A champion swimmer might have a deadly encounter with a shark one day. An Olympic athlete ages—it's a fact of life. A professional football player may end up with a shattered kneecap, and so on.

Scan to watch Pharrell's speech at NYU's 185th commencement in May 2017

Pharrell lives for music but also has many other passions. He's created several clothing companies, started and maintained a successful YouTube channel, acted in films and in TV series, and helped organize a very successful after-school and summer camp program for underprivileged kids.

Organization

This busy artist is extremely structured, with a set time each day for phone calls, public relations work, and so on, and a set time when he enters his studio to work. He also applies strict limits to be sure he has time that is purely for his family, and keeps that side of his life as private as he can. That's obvious by the fact that nine months after his triplets were born, their names have not been released.

Happy makes Pharrell Williams cry (interview with Oprah)

Humility

No matter what is going on in the world or with his career, Pharrell chooses to keep an open mind and remain humble. He is always ready and eager to collaborate and has worked with people from all walks of life and from all ethnicities around the globe.

Be Happy

In October 2017, Pharrell was interviewed by a seven-year-old Canadian girl named Poppy for the "Little W" internet segment of *W Magazine*.

"What are five things that make you 'happy'?" the charming little redhead asked.

"Number one, God or the Universe," Pharrell answered. "Number two, my family. Number three, my job. Making music. Number four, people recognizing that empathy is the only way we can move forward as a species. Number five, seeing other people happy."

Pharrell and Ellen discuss the importance of love and acceptance

Text-Dependent Questions:

❶ What is the name of the sneakers created by Pharrell's newest collaboration with Adidas?

❷ What is the name of Pharrell's YouTube channel?

❸ Name three ways that Pharrell uses to get messages across to his audience.

Research Project:

Do a Google search for "Pharrell Williams lyrics." Choose two songs written by Pharrell and discuss the lyrics. What is he saying to his audience?

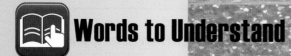

Words to Understand

amenable: a person who is responsive and open to suggestion; one who is agreeable and can be easily persuaded.

lymphomas: a group of blood cancers that come from and affect the white blood cells in our immune system that help our bodies fight disease.

nationalists: people who have very strong patriotic feelings, who usually believe that their country is superior to all other countries.

philanthropist: a generous person who is concerned for the welfare of others and wants to help, often by donating money, work, or property to those in need.

trajectory: the path of an object through space, like a missile.

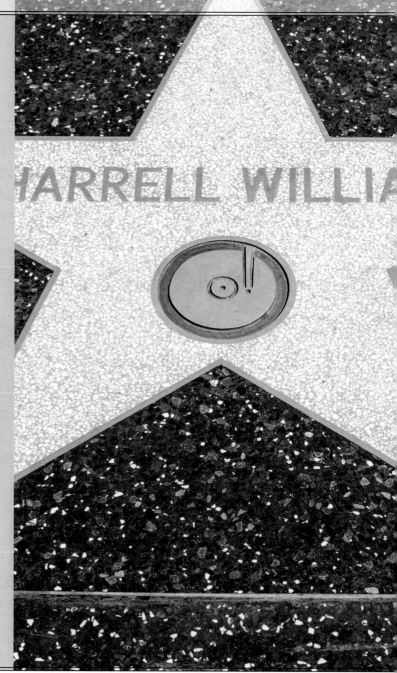

Chapter 5:

Giving Back to the Community to Make a Difference

Charitable Activities

From One Hand to AnOTHER (FOHTA)

In 2008, Pharrell created FOHTA to help underserved children and teens be exposed to different cultures and different ways of thinking, and receive the time and opportunity to learn new and exciting concepts. He believes that if a child is encouraged and has the right tools to work with, they can be successful in life.

FOHTA currently runs three free after-school programs and Summer of Innovation camps at sixteen different locations in two states. The current focus of these camps is STEM education—science, technology, engineering, and math. Since its creation, FOHTA has been affiliated with NASA, and the collaboration between astronauts and scientists has been an incredible learning experience for everyone involved.

Dr. Carolyn Williams, Pharrell's mother, serves as director of education and chairwoman of the board of FOHTA. She estimates that approximately 3,000 students are helped each year. A recently added component of their after-school hands-on program is called "Think Green." It teaches students about the new three R's—not Reading, 'Riting, and 'Rithmetic, but Reducing, Recycling, and Reusing. FOHTA's mission is to "change the world one kid at a time by giving them the tools and resources to meet their potential."

Gabrielle's Angel Foundation for Cancer Research

Intelligent and beautiful, Switzerland-born Gabrielle Rich Aouad spoke five languages and was an expert horseback rider and champion skier when first diagnosed with a very advanced case of Hodgkin's **lymphoma** at the age of twenty-three. She beat it and went on to move to the United States, get married, and star in seven movies and eight plays.

Sadly, the cancer came back twice more, the last episode requiring a bone marrow transplant from her mother. It was not successful, and she passed away at the age of twenty-seven. Her final wish was to create a foundation that would research different treatments for leukemia. The treatments she and other patients experienced were unpleasant, forcing her to cope with the damage and side effects of radiation and chemotherapy.

Usher

Pharrell is very interested in this cause, and has donated time and money. He performed with Usher at the annual Angel Ball on

October 29, 2013, in New York City. This is also a favorite cause of the Kardashian family, who donated $250,000 in 2016 in honor of their father, who died from esophageal cancer.

The Angel Foundation supports basic scientific and innovative clinical research to find new therapies for patients with lymphoma, leukemia, and other related cancers. It also funds research that studies current treatments to improve their effectiveness, reduce their poisonous or toxic effects, and help enhance the quality of life of all the patients who suffer from these diseases.

Get Schooled Foundation

This non-profit organization, founded in the United States in 2010 by the Bill and Melinda Gates Foundation and Viacom, uses the power of popular culture, technology, and the media to both inspire and motivate teenagers, their teachers, and their families. The goal is to raise the rate of high school graduation and to increase the number of students who go to college. It works with both middle school and high school pupils to improve attendance numbers by becoming involved with an individual student's need for financial aid, as well as providing a large number of grants and scholarships.

Pharrell got involved with the organization in 2011 by headlining the Get Schooled Tour and National Challenge along with Ludacris. They rode buses to major cities—like Los Angeles, Chicago, and New York—to speak with students, parents, and teachers about the importance of education.

Got Your 6

"Got Your 6" is military speak for "I've got your back." This organization, which started in 2012 in Washington, DC, empowers returning veterans to work with their communities and to be able to employ the leadership skills they learned in the military. The foundation also interacts with Hollywood, encouraging the increased display of the positive attributes of returning veterans—instead of stereotyping them as either Rambo-like heroes or broken individuals suffering from PTSD (post-traumatic stress disorder).

This organization was inspired by the collaboration of then First Lady Michelle Obama and the entertainment industry. Pharrell joined with Tom Hanks, Alec Baldwin, Sarah Jessica Parker, and many other celebrities in creating an important PSA (public service announcement) to make more communities aware of the important goals of Got Your 6.

Indigenous Environmental Network

This U.S. organization, started in 1990, supports indigenous peoples (sometimes called First Nation peoples or Native Americans) who are working together to protect Mother Earth from exploitation and contamination. Funds are used to assist these groups preserve sacred sites, natural resources (water, land, air), and the health of all living things. This is achieved by organizing direct action campaigns, building public awareness and a sense of community, and creating alliances between ethnic and people-of-color organizations, women and youth groups, labor groups, environmental organizations, and many others.

Pharrell Williams, along with Leonardo DiCaprio and Bernie Sanders, have all contributed financially to this important organization.

PowHERful®

Pharrell also serves on the board of this New York City–based organization. It was started in 2001 by Soledad O'Brien and her husband, Brad Raymond, and provides mentorship and financial assistance to young women so they can attend and graduate from college.

Benefit Concerts

Pharrell has appeared in many charitable performances over the years. Most recently, he sang with Justin Timberlake, the Dave Matthews Band, Ariana Grande, Coldplay, Stevie Wonder, and others at "A Concert for Charlottesville" on September 24, 2017. Donations were collected for victims of white supremacist protestors who fought against counter-demonstrators in Charlottesville, Virginia, on August 11–12. The funds were also distributed to first responders and for any organizations who promote unity, healing, and justice— both locally and nationwide. A final tally of how much money was collected has not been released.

Pharrell also performed alongside Ariana Grande, Justin Bieber, and the Black Eyed Peas before a crowd of fifty thousand at the "One Love Show" in Manchester, England, on June 03, 2017. Funds raised by

Coldplay

this concert event benefitted the victims of a terrorist bomb attack in Manchester on May 22, which left 22 people dead and over 100 injured. The event raised over £10 million pounds for victims and their families.

On a Humble Note

Tyson Toussant, the co-founder of Bionic Yarn and who works closely with Pharrell, had this to say to Sean Stormes. He was doing research for a 2014 article in the *Kansas City Business Journal*.

> *[Pharrell] has every right to an inflated ego, but he's extra humble … It has to do with the way he was raised. He's a very **amenable** Southern gentleman. He calls everyone sir or ma'am. I grew up in Manhattan, and there are friends of mine, you'd think they had invented Twitter. He's not like that. He'll treat a doorman and Bill Gates the same way.*

In My Mind Setback

When Pharrell's first solo album debuted in 2006, he realized that there was too much ego involved with it.

[In My Mind] didn't turn out the way I wanted it to, and I blamed everybody around me but myself. I really had to take a long study on what I was doing and talking about on that record … I realized along the way that there wasn't enough purpose in my music. Listening to Stevie Wonder and Steely Dan songs, you'd see that Donald Fagen had a purpose—an intention.

What Pharrell learned was that he wants his music to be uplifting to people, and at the same time, he wants to remain humble. When asked whether he thought it was dangerous to take too much personal credit for success, he replied,

> You see people spin out of control all the time. Those are the most tragic stories; the most gifted people who start to believe it's really all them. It's not all you. Just like you need air to fly a kite, it's not the kite. It's the air. **"**

Fighting against Racism

On a VH1 show on September 18, 2017—*Hip Hop Honors: The 90's Game Changers*—Pharrell delivered a very powerful speech in which he denounced white **nationalists** and called on everyone to act against racism. His powerful speech continued with these words.

> Don't think just because they're coming at the African Americans and they're coming at the Jewish community and they're coming at the Hispanics that it can't be you, just 'cos you look like them. They're using you … You should understand that they could change their minds, and it might not be about black, white, big, skinny, or small. It might be about facial features, it might be about hair color. Don't act like they didn't do that before … The white nationalists are walking towards your future. What you gonna do? **"**

Scan the code to watch Pharrell Williams warning against being fooled by injustice (the extended speech)

Fighting against Sexism

Pharrell grew up with a mother who was very involved with both literacy and education, and he has always spoken out in favor of the empowerment of women. In an interview in January 2017, Pharrell said,

> I don't know what I could do, but I know if women wanted to, they could save this nation. If women wanted to, they could save the world.

Pharrell has stated that his G I R L album was a "twenty-first-century take on feminism." Most recently, he wrote and produced the film *Hidden Figures*, which brings to attention the previously untold true story of three brilliant African-American women scientists who played a very important role while working at NASA. They calculated flight **trajectories** and crunched data for the space program, working as "human computers" in a segregated area of the Langley Research Center in Virginia.

In this film, Pharrell shines a light on these women and gives them the credit they so richly deserve.

Actress Octavia Spencer, who plays Dorothy Vaughan in the film Hidden Figures *speaks at the premiere of the film after a reception to honor NASA's "human computers" on Thursday, Dec. 1, 2016, at the Virginia Air and Space Center in Hampton, VA.* Hidden Figures *stars Taraji P. Henson as Katherine Johnson, the African-American mathematician, physicist, and space scientist who calculated flight trajectories for John Glenn's first orbital flight in 1962.*

Text-Dependent Questions:

❶ Name two benefit concerts that Pharrell has taken part in recently.

❷ What does the organization Got Your 6 address?

❸ What are three things that make Pharrell happy, according to an interview he gave to a seven-year-old girl named Poppy?

Research Project:

Pharrell has had a very successful career as a writer, singer, composer, producer, actor, fashion designer, and entrepreneur. He also had a nurturing childhood and is now the father of four small children. A **philanthropist** at heart, he has created an organization to help underserved children and teenagers receive much-needed encouragement with their educations and future possible careers. In addition, he supports many other charitable foundations.

For this project, select two of the non-profit charities Pharrell has started or contributed to. Write a paper that discusses these organizations and what they stand for. Finally, choose a charitable organization that is not mentioned here that you would like to support, and explain why this charity is your choice.

Series Glossary of Key Terms

A&R: an abbreviation that stands for Artists and Repertoire, which is a record company department responsible for the recruitment and development of talent; similar to a talent scout for sports.

ambient: a musical style that relies on electronic sounds, gentle music, and the lack of a regular beat to create a relaxed mood for the listener.

brand: a particular product or a characteristic that serves to identify a particular product; a brand name is one having a well-known and usually highly regarded or marketable word or phrase.

cameo: also called a cameo role; a minor part played by a prominent performer in a single scene of a motion picture or a television show.

choreography: the art of planning and arranging the movements, steps, and patterns of dancers.

collaboration: a product created by working with someone else; combining individual talents.

debut: a first public appearance on a stage, on television, or so on, or the beginning of a profession or career; the first appearance of something, like a new product.

deejay (DJ): a slang term for a person who spins vinyl records on a turntable; aka a disc jockey.

demo: a recording of a new song, or of one performed by an unknown singer or group, distributed to disc jockeys, recording companies, and the like, to demonstrate the merits of the song or performer.

dubbed: something that is named or given a new name or title; in movies, when the actors' voices have been replaced with those of different performers speaking another language; in music, transfer or copying of previously recorded audio material from one medium to another.

endorsement: money earned from a product recommendation, typically by a celebrity, athlete, or other public figure.

entrepreneur: a person who organizes and manages any enterprise, especially a business, usually with considerable initiative and at financial risk.

falsetto: a man singing in an unnaturally high voice, accomplished by creating a vibration at the very edge of the vocal chords.

genre: a subgroup or category within a classification, typically associated with works of art, such as music or literature.

hone, honing: sharpening or refining a set of skills necessary to achieve success or perform a specific task.

icon: a symbol that represents something, such as a team, a religious person, a location, or an idea.

innovation: the introduction of something new or different; a brand-new feature or upgrade to an existing idea, method, or item.

instrumental: serving as a crucial means, agent, or tool; of, relating to, or done with an instrument or tool.

jingle: a short verse, tune, or slogan used in advertising to make a product easily remembered.

mogul: someone considered to be very important, powerful, and in charge; a term usually associated with heads of businesses in the television, movie studio, or recording industries.

performing arts: skills that require public performance, as acting, singing, or dancing.

philanthropy: goodwill to fellow members of the human race; an active effort to promote human welfare.

public relations: the activity or job of providing information about a particular person or organization to the public so that people will regard that person or organization in a favorable way.

sampler: a digital or electronic musical instrument, related to a synthesizer, that uses samples, or sound recordings, of real instruments (trumpet, violin, piano, etc.) mixed with excerpts of recorded songs and other interesting sounds (sirens, ocean waves, construction noises, car horns, etc.) that are stored digitally and can be replayed by a triggering device, like a sequencer, electronic drums, or a MIDI keyboard.

single: a music recording having two or more tracks that is shorter than an album, EP, or LP; also, a song that is particularly popular, independent of other songs on the same album or by the same artist.

Further Reading

Gilliam, Nathaniel. *The Pharrell Williams Handbook*. Queensland, Australia: Emereo Publishing Pty Ltd, 2016.

Lester, Paul. *In Search of Pharrell Williams*. London: Omnibus Press, 2015.

Roberts, Chris. *Pharrell Williams: Blurring the Lines*. Carlton Books, Carlton Publishing Group: London, 2016.

Uhl, Xina M. *Pharrell Williams: Music Industry Star*. Momentum, The Child's World, Inc., 2017.

Williams, Pharrell. *Happy!* New York: G.P. Putnam's Sons Books for Young Readers, 2015.

Williams, Pharrell. *Pharrell: Places and Spaces I've Been*. New York: Rizzoli, 2012.

Internet Resources

http://www.billboard.com/
The official site of Billboard Music contains lists and charts that track the most popular albums and singles.

https://www.hotnewhiphop.com/articles/news/
HotNewHipHop contains the latest news on your favorite hip-hop artists, including Pharrell!

http://pharrellwilliams.com/
Pharrell William's personal website features an interactive approach, combining news about Pharrell with links to his fans' favorite projects.

http://www.recordingmag.com/
Recording, the Magazine for the Recording Musician features reviews, quotes, resources, and videos.

http://www.rollingstone.com/music
Rolling Stone magazine has been at the forefront of music news since 1967.

Educational Video Links

Chapter 1:
http://x-qr.net/1GpA
http://x-qr.net/1GQ7
http://x-qr.net/1Hkz
http://x-qr.net/1DwE
http://x-qr.net/1DCs
http://x-qr.net/1D9z
http://x-qr.net/1H68
http://x-qr.net/1GpU
http://x-qr.net/1GPj
http://x-qr.net/1CzC

Chapter 2:
http://x-qr.net/1GZr
http://x-qr.net/1HqQ
http://x-qr.net/1Gsk

Chapter 3:
http://x-qr.net/1F7e
http://x-qr.net/1E0k

Chapter 4:
http://x-qr.net/1Eqh
http://x-qr.net/1GDS
http://x-qr.net/1GU4

Chapter 5:
http://x-qr.net/1HST

Citations

"We're the ones playing the instruments…" by Chad Hugo. Patel, Joseph. "N.E.R.D. Step Up Their Game on Fly or Die, Reminisce about Teen Years." *MTV News*. December 09, 2003.

"So we thought why not make a timeless album…" by Pharrell Williams. Graff, Gary. "Pharrell Describes New NE*R*D Album as a Time Capsule." *Billboard*. October 12, 2010.

"It wasn't, like, third world poverty…" by David Williams. Lester, Paul. "The Hit Man." *The Guardian*. February 19, 2004.

"Don't hire him! He burns…" by a former McDonald's manager. "23 Amazing Facts You Didn't Know about Pharrell Williams." CapitalXTRA.com. 2017.

"Growing up, Williams had no interest…" by Mary Kaye Schilling, interviewing Pharrell Williams for her article entitled, "Get Busy: Pharrell's Productivity Secrets." FastCompany.com. November 18, 2013.

"It just always stuck out…" by Pharrell Williams in an interview for ABC-TV's *Nightline*. "Pharrell Williams: Tasting the Universe." 2012.

"You like the drums, so…" by Pharrell's grandmother. NPR Staff. "Pharrell Williams On Juxtaposition and Seeing Sounds." *The Record, NPR Music News*, heard on *Morning Edition* show. December 31, 2013.

"No, sir, I don't know…" by Pharrell Williams. Sin, Ben. "Pharrell Williams Interview." *Time Out Magazine* (Kuala Lumpur). [n.d.]

"This 2004 Snoop Dogg cut brought…" by ETCanada.com (*Entertainment Tonight News* television show) Staff. ET Canada Digital. "Pharrell's Best Guest Appearances." December 19, 2014.

"People's energies are made of their souls…" by Pharrell Williams. Net Music Countdown with David Lawrence. NetMusicCountdown.com. [n.d.]

"…feather-light vocal style…" by Monarch. *Monarch*. "15 of the Best Falsettos in Music Right Now." July 10, 2013.

"Most anything I do I do because…" Schilling, "Get Busy…" 2013.

"A cultural movement dedicated to Thinkers…" by Pharrell Williams, describing his YouTube channel *i am Other*. May 15, 2012.

"[The Billionaire Boys Club] was born in Japan…" by Pharrell Williams. Blagrove, Kadia, Joe La Puma and Jian DeLeon. "The Oral History of Billionaire Boys Club and Ice Cream." Complex.com. December 03, 2013.

"[Pharrell] has every right to…" Schilling, "Get Busy…" 2013.

"It's made with 26,000 diamonds…" by Pharrell Williams. Russeth, Andrew, quoting *Bloomberg* interview in 2009. "That $2 M. Sculpture by Pharrell, Murakami, and Jacob the Jeweler Is in Miami." Observer.com. December 08, 2012.

"How can we inspire …" by Pharrell Williams. "Interview with Pharrell Williams." Pirelli.com. March 08, 2017.

"Newness, freshness, and what-is-that-ness…" by Pharrell Williams. Muller, Marissa G. "Pharrell Williams, Justin Timberlake and Cara Delevingne Nerd out over Alabama Shakes." TheFader.com. July 04, 2015.

"Speaking to you guys today…" by Pharrell Williams. *Time* Staff. "Pharrell Williams at NYU Graduation: 'Imagine the Possibilities When We Remove Imbalance.'" *Time* (magazine). May 17, 2017.

"They tried to put us in…" by Pharrell Williams. "Pharrell Williams Performs 'Freedom' at MTV VMAs 2015." Just Jared.com. August 30, 2015.

"If you see the potential for good…" by Pharrell Williams. Twitter. August 26, 2017.

"What are five things that make…" by Poppy Browne. Darmon, Aynslee. "Pharrell Chats with 7-Year-Old about What Makes Him 'Happy.'" ETCanada.com. October 02, 2017.

"Change the world one kid…" by FOHTA. From One Hand to AnOTHER home page. http://fohta.org/ Accessed November 27, 2017.

"[Pharrell] has every right to…" by Sean Stormes. "Pharrell Williams—Producer, Performer, Philosopher." *Kansas City Business Journal*. April 18, 2014.

"It didn't turn out the way…" Stormes, "Pharrell Williams…" 2014.

"You see people spin…" Stormes, "Pharrell Williams…" 2014.

"Don't think just because…" by Pharrell Williams. Bowman, Lisa. "Pharrell Urges Fans to Take Action against Racism in Moving 'Hip Hop Honors' Speech." September 19, 2017.

"I don't know what I could…" by Pharrell. Hitching-Hales, James. "'Women Could Save the World': Pharrell Williams Shows His Feminist Side in Interview." GlobalCitizen.org. January 19, 2017.

"Human computers…" by 20th Century Fox. Plot summary for *Hidden Figures*. IMDb.com. January 06, 2017.

Photo Credits

Chapter 1:
ID 22659837 © Featureflash | Dreamstime
ID 9089446 © Aaron Settipane | Dreamstime
ID 22441759 © Komelau | Dreamstime
ID 22659837 © Featureflash | Dreamstime
ID 23229635 © Laurence Agron | Dreamstime
ID 25588276 © Featureflash | Dreamstime
ID 26358200 © Carrienelson1 | Dreamstime
ID 45217877 © Jaguarps | Dreamstime
ID 45536950 © Jaguarps | Dreamstime
ID 47627826 © Turkbug | Dreamstime
ID 58738985 © Starstock | Dreamstime
ID 103366465 © Christian Bertrand | Dreamstime

Chapter 2:
Chadhugo_(300dpi).jpg | ©Seher Sikandar | Wikimedia Commons
ID 53521795 © Starstock | Dreamstime
ID 102655529 © Christian Bertrand | Dreamstime

Chapter 3:
Pharrell.jpg | Wikimedia Commons
N.E.R.D.jpg | Wikimedia Commons
Sean_Combs_2.jpg | Wikimedia Commons

Channel_headquarters_bordercropped.jpg | Wikimedia Commons
ID 27559790 © Roystudio | Dreamstime
ID 34073910 © Little_prince | Dreamstime
ID 35296249 © Ivan Mikhaylov | Dreamstime
ID 24618043 © Sbukley | Dreamstime
ID 25133755 © Sbukley | Dreamstime
D 48961194 © Jaguarps | Dreamstime
D 56332563 © Mrchan | Dreamstime

Chapter 4:
#39475170 | ©Aliaksandr Dobysh | Fotolia
ID 22767245 © Sbukley | Dreamstime
ID 24036425 © Sbukley | Dreamstime
ID 30012322 © Sbukley | Dreamstime
ID 52074195 © Mirko Vitali | Dreamstime
ID 55692239 © Starstock | Dreamstime

Chapter 5:
NHQ201612010033).jpg | NASA | Wikimedia Commons
ID 38421348 © Pixelrobot | Dreamstime
ID 23572711 © Sbukley | Dreamstime
ID 25374159 © Featureflash | Dreamstime
D 26355734 © Sbukley | Dreamstime

Index

Index

Index

Author's Biography

Lori Vetere is a graduate of the University of Pittsburgh and has traveled all over Central and South America. She loves books, learning, music, traveling, and new opportunities. Learn more at https://www.writeraccess.com/clients/writers-view/12784.